How to Shake the World With $100

Roger Hertzler

CHRISTIAN LIGHT

PUBLICATIONS

HOW TO SHAKE THE WORLD WITH ONE HUNDRED DOLLARS

Christian Light Publications

Harrisonburg, Virginia 22802

©2020 Christian Light Publications, Inc.

Printed in the United States of America

ISBN: 978-0-87813-317-8

Cover & Interior Design:
D. Brandon Hartman

Cover & Interior Graphics:
Getty Images & Christian Light

Contents

Foreword

The purpose of this book is to challenge us. I recognize, though, that with any challenge, there is a high risk of not being perfectly balanced. There is usually a ditch on both sides of the road.

So while I want to challenge us to look at our giving as a very real, very necessary, and very powerful ministry, I do not want to de-emphasize other necessary things such as going as missionaries, praying for the lost, or witnessing to others one-on-one. While I want to challenge us to target our giving where the needs are the greatest, I do not want to give us license to neglect our first responsibilities of paying

our own bills and the bills of our local congregations. While I want to challenge us to consider carefully how God wants us to use our money, I do not want to encourage a judgmental spirit toward others who do it differently.

The reality is that none of us, individuals or churches, will do it exactly the same. But can I still encourage you to accept the challenge and joyfully obey the Lord Jesus with all you have, including the money He's entrusted to you? After all, we are His servants, called to promote His cause and to build His kingdom.

Chapter 1
From Greenland's Icy Mountains

The largest island in the world is **Greenland**. It has a population of around 55,000, which is about the same as Albany, Oregon, the city where I was born. This might not seem like a lot of people; but think about the fact that all of these people need Jesus. If we could share the Gospel with ten people per day, it would take us well over fifteen years to reach everyone in Greenland.

That may seem like a large task, but it would be an even bigger task to evangelize the island of **Guam** in the western Pacific. This little island has over three times the population of Greenland, at nearly 165,000 people. And these people all need Jesus too.

However, even Guam's population is small compared to the Central American country of **Belize**. This country has a population of around 375,000 people, which is more than double the population of Guam. And all these people also need Jesus.

The population of Belize, however, is small compared to the country of **Bhutan** in southern Asia. With over 800,000 people, Bhutan has more people than the countries of Belize, Guam, and Greenland together.

However, Bhutan is also small when compared to the country of **Bahrain** in western Asia. With a population of nearly 1.5 million, Bahrain has more people than Bhutan, Belize, Guam, and Greenland together. Every one of these people also needs Jesus.

Even bigger than Bahrain is the country of **Mongolia** in eastern Asia. With a population of over 3 million, Mongolia has more people than Bahrain, Bhutan, Belize, Guam, and Greenland together.

Mongolia might seem like it has a lot of people, but it also is small when compared to the country of **Nicaragua** in Central America. With well over 6 million people, Nicaragua has more people than Mongolia, Bahrain, Bhutan, Belize, Guam, and Greenland together.

However, even Nicaragua is small when compared with the country of **Somalia** in eastern Africa. Somalia has a population of nearly 15 million, which makes it bigger than Nicaragua, Mongolia, Bahrain, Bhutan, Belize, Guam, and Greenland together. And each one of these people needs Jesus.

Although Somalia certainly has a lot of people, it doesn't have nearly as many people as the country of **Nepal** in southern Asia. Nepal's population is over 29 million, and therefore has more people than Somalia, Nicaragua, Mongolia, Bahrain, Bhutan, Belize, Guam, and Greenland together.

There is another large country in eastern Africa called **Tanzania**. Tanzania has over 57 million people, making it bigger than Nepal, Somalia, Nicaragua, Mongolia, Bahrain, Bhutan, Belize, Guam, and Greenland together. Every one of these people in Tanzania needs Jesus.

Tanzania might seem like a huge country, and it is. However, there is a country in the western hemisphere that has over twice the population of Tanzania. This country is **Mexico**, the tenth most populous country in the world. The population of Mexico, at over 129 million people, is more than the populations of Tanzania, Nepal, Somalia, Nicaragua, Mongolia, Bahrain, Bhutan, Belize, Guam, and Greenland together.

Although the population of Mexico is huge, it is small in comparison to the population of **Indonesia**, the fourth-largest country in the world. Indonesia has a population of nearly

3

264 million people, which is more than Mexico, Tanzania, Nepal, Somalia, Nicaragua, Mongolia, Bahrain, Bhutan, Belize, Guam, and Greenland together. And all these people need Jesus.

Although the population of Indonesia is truly mind-boggling, the population of the country of **India** is much, much larger. With a population of well over 1.3 billion people, India has more people than Indonesia, Mexico, Tanzania, Nepal, Somalia, Nicaragua, Mongolia, Bahrain, Bhutan, Belize, Guam, and Greenland together. In fact, if you would add the populations of all these other countries together, it would not even come to one-half of the population of India.

To get a country with the population equal to that of India, we would have to take all the people from the twelve countries listed above, and then add to them the 144 million people who live in the country of **Russia**. Russia is the largest country in the world by area, and the ninth-largest country by population, putting it just ahead of Mexico. But even that would not be enough to get us to the population of India, so we would also have to add in the 165 million people from **Bangladesh**. (This country has a land area smaller than the state of Iowa, but it has a population larger than the country of Russia.)

But even the population of Bangladesh would not bump us up to the population of India, so we would also need to add in the population of **Brazil**, which has the fifth-largest population in the world at well over 200 million people. Finally, we would need to also throw in the 325 million people from the third most populous nation, which is the **United States of America**. Only then would we have a group of people approaching the size of the population of India.

Now that you are starting to grasp the staggering number of people that live in India, please consider several important facts.

Fact 1: All the people in India need Jesus.

Fact 2: The country of China has just as many people, or even slightly more, than India does.

Fact 3: All the people in China need Jesus.

Fact 4: There are around 3.5 billion people, or nearly half of the world's population, who live in countries other than India, China, or any of the other countries already mentioned.

Fact 5: All the people in the world need Jesus.

Jesus commanded us as His followers to go into all the world and preach the Gospel to every person.

This is starting to look a little overwhelming.

Chapter 2
They Shook
the World

Every one of the world's 7.5 billion people has needs, the greatest of which is the need to know Jesus. But every person also has influence, meaning that each of us is having some sort of an impact on the people around us. For some of us, this influence might seem negligible. Others, however, have had an enormous influence; they have made such a difference that the world truly will never be the same.

Recently I did an online search for "the most influential people of all time." The resulting list included people who shook the world with evil, such as Stalin, Hitler, and Pol Pot. It included people who shook the world through their scientific discoveries, such as Newton, Einstein, and Galileo. It included people who shook the world through their inventions, such as Gutenberg, Edison, and Alexander Graham

Bell. And it included those who shook their world through their military conquests, such as Alexander the Great, George Washington, and Napoleon.

These people all left their mark on humanity, and this world has never been the same since.

But I was especially interested in learning about those who had made a difference for Jesus Christ and His kingdom. After all, the world's greatest need is not for philosophy, scientific discoveries, or military conquests. The world's greatest need is Jesus, the Lamb of God who takes away the sin of the world.

Jesus told His followers to "seek ye first the kingdom of God," and Paul writes that we should "seek those things which are above." Christ's kingdom is glorious, it is powerful, and it is eternal. By inviting us to seek His kingdom, He is inviting us to join a cause and to participate in a program that will never pass away.

Whether they are recorded in history books or not, Christ had followers in every generation who made a difference for His kingdom. These were a rare breed of passionate souls who lived with their eyes on the "great beyond." They include those who shook the world through their preaching, such as John Wesley, Dwight Moody, and George Brunk. They include those who shook the world through their prayers, such as David Brainerd, George Mueller, and John Hyde. They include those who shook the world through their missionary endeavors, such as Adoniram Judson, Hudson Taylor, and Ralph Palmer.

While those listed above all achieved some level of fame through their efforts for God's kingdom, there are many who labored faithfully for Christ for years without ever becoming famous. Such workers do not seek to receive glory from men, but they still are shaking the world for Christ. Meanwhile, their heavenly Father, who sees in secret, is making plans to reward them openly.

Are you willing to be one of them?

Chapter 3
What Are You Doing Today?

Seek ye first the kingdom of God, and his righteousness; and all these things shall be added unto you.
— Matthew 6:33

In response to Jesus' command in Matthew 6:33, every child of God should have, deep within his soul, a burning desire to make a difference for Christ and His kingdom. Most of us, however, do not wake up on an average morning with the opportunity to preach to the multitudes like Dwight Moody, to travel to Burma like Adoniram Judson, or to spend the whole day praying like John Hyde.

Instead, many of us wake up on a normal morning having already committed, either explicitly or implicitly, that we will "go to work" today. In other words, we will spend a large part of our day trading our time, talents, and efforts for cold, hard cash. That sounds pretty carnal, doesn't it? Is there any chance for us to be used by God today when we will be spending so much of our time in this way?

The answer is a resounding yes. In fact, it is precisely *because* we spend so much of our time working in a fairly well-paying job that we have an amazing opportunity to shake the world for Jesus.

The danger is that many of us are missing it.

The challenge to all of us who are reading this book is this: Let's not miss it. Let's wake up and recognize that if we are average Christians living in North America, we have opportunities to shake the world for Jesus. And we can do it starting right now.

But to do that, most of us need a change in perspective, a radical transformation in how we view an ordinary day of work.

To illustrate how this change of mind could develop and how it could impact our thinking, let me introduce you to five brothers. All five are professing Christians, and we will call them Andrew, Brian, Caleb, David, and Edward. Come with me and observe the different ways they approach an ordinary day of work and the opportunities that come with it.

Chapter 4
Andrew
the Slothful

On his first day of work, Andrew certainly intended to get out of bed when his alarm rang the first time. He discovered, however, that it was much easier to stay in bed another forty-five minutes, so that is what he did. This decision forced him to rush to try to make it to work on time, but alas, he failed. For a good part of his workday he was still trying to wake up, and for the rest of his workday he was looking forward to quitting time. When quitting time finally arrived, he was the first person out the door and on his way home to take a much-needed nap.

This approach to his workday soon became a way of life for Andrew. Since he was usually the last person to arrive at work and the first person to leave, and since he didn't seem too excited about working while he was there, Andrew's boss gave him only the easiest jobs and saved the more challenging assignments, the promotions, and the pay raises for others. At first he offered Andrew some opportunities to work overtime, but Andrew always turned them down, and his boss finally stopped offering.

Because of his approach to work, Andrew's income always remained lower than average for the young men his age. He continually found it difficult to keep up with his bills, and he never had quite enough money for the things he wanted to do. He couldn't understand why other people always seemed to have more money than he did, and he spent a good deal of time dropping subtle complaints about that fact. But whenever anyone would cautiously suggest that there might be a connection between his level of income and his attitude about work, he could usually come up with a fairly good reason why that was not the case. Then he would go back to his subtle complaining.

Chapter 5
Brian
the Worker

As Brian observed Andrew's life, he decided he would do things differently. He was not impressed with Andrew's slothfulness, and he certainly didn't like the idea of always being so short on cash.

Also, Brian knew just enough about the Bible to know that laziness was not a good thing. Numerous verses from Proverbs, as well as various passages from the New Testament, lifted up the virtues of hard work and warned strongly against laziness. For instance, he knew 1 Thessalonians 4:11 contains the command to "work with your own hands," and 2 Thessalonians 3:10 says "if any would not work, neither should he eat."

So when Brian's alarm rang early Monday morning, he jumped right out of bed, grabbed a bite to eat, and was one of the first ones to arrive at work. All day he put his heart into his work, trying to learn everything he could about the business and looking for ways to get more accomplished in the time he had. When the end of the day came, Brian was the first one to volunteer to work overtime, and, sure enough, his foreman took him up on his offer.

Brian's diligence in work soon grabbed the attention of the boss, and it wasn't long before he was offered a new position as foreman, along with a generous raise to his hourly pay rate. With these changes, Brian's income was soon nearly $100 higher per day than that of his brother Andrew, and most of this difference was a direct result of his different attitude about work.

Because of this additional income, Brian was able to enjoy a lifestyle Andrew could only dream of. He was able to wear nicer clothes, eat finer foods, and enjoy more extravagant vacations. Although by the end of the month he usually would not have any extra money in his bank account, he could always remember with pleasure all the fun he had had in spending the extra cash he had earned.

Chapter 6
Caleb
the Saver

Caleb looked at his older brother Brian with a degree of admiration and decided to emulate him in his work ethic. Sure enough, as he began to make some of the same choices as Brian, he also began to experience some of the same results. His boss took notice, he received some promotions, and soon, like Brian, he was earning around $100 more per day than their brother Andrew.

However, there was something about Brian's life that always bothered Caleb. This was the fact that even though Brian was earning more money than Andrew, at the end of the day, he really didn't have anything to show for it. It occurred to Caleb that Brian seemed to be living only for the present, and that he didn't think at all about what might happen in the future.

Caleb observed that the truly wise men around him were those who lived not just for the present, but also for the future, and he decided to do the same. So instead of spending his extra money on a higher lifestyle like Brian did, he opened a savings account and began putting his extra money into it. The balance in Caleb's savings account grew rapidly, and before long he was moving money to other types of investments that generated higher rates of return.

By doing some calculations based on the incredible power of compound interest, Caleb was soon able to determine that he was well on his way to becoming a wealthy man at a relatively young age, and he felt certain that his future was going to be well provided for.

Chapter 7
David
the Giver

As David observed the examples of his older brothers, he began to develop some convictions accordingly. First, he decided he didn't want to be lazy like Andrew, but rather wanted to be diligent like Brian and Caleb. Second, rather than living only for the present like Andrew and Brian, he wanted to be a person who lived for the future like Caleb. If he was going to spend so much of his time working, he wanted to have something to show for it at the end of the day.

Soon he, too, was working hard, getting promotions, and earning far more than he needed to live on. Before long he was ready to move his first $100 from checking to savings, following the example of Caleb, the brother that he admired the most. But then David began to ponder something that had never occurred to him before.

Although he admired Caleb for his hard work, disciplined spending, and future-oriented thinking, he began to wonder how secure all these investments were that Caleb was making. He knew Caleb tended to stick with more "conservative" investments and that he protected his investments with adequate insurance when appropriate. However, there seemed to be one thing that Caleb was missing. This was the fact that at any moment, all of Caleb's wealth could be snatched from his grasp by that universal enemy called death. Although Caleb's wealth looked secure, the truth was that none of it really was secure.

Then David began to consider more closely the teachings of Jesus and discovered that Jesus had warned about the insecurity of earthly investments and had commanded us instead to invest our extra resources in Heaven, where we could keep them for all eternity. There they would be impervious to the risks of fire, inflation, moths, rust, and thieves.

Upon further study, David discovered that the way Jesus told us we could lay up our treasure in Heaven was through giving to charity. He decided then and there he was going to be obedient to his Lord's command and lay up his treasure in Heaven rather than on earth.

That Sunday David took his $100 to church and dropped it into the offering basket. It didn't occur to him to check into what the offering that day was going to be used for, since he figured it really was not his business.

As it turned out, the offering that Sunday happened to be going toward the building fund for a new sanctuary, and David's $100 eventually went to purchase several square feet of carpet and a brass doorknob.

Chapter 8
Edward
the Shaker

The fifth and final brother, Edward, had plenty of examples to choose from as he began his working career. He immediately rejected the slothfulness of Andrew in favor of the diligence of Brian. He rejected Brian's undisciplined spending in favor of Caleb's future-oriented saving. And when he heard David explain that giving to charity is an investment rather than an expense, and a way to lay up our wealth in Heaven rather than here on earth, Edward decided that this was what he wanted to do also.

But when it came time to "invest" the first $100 he had available, Edward decided to pause, think, and ask himself a few questions. *If I am going to lay up treasures in Heaven, does it make any difference where I give my money? If I am going to lay up treasures in Heaven, does Jesus care at all about who the recipients of my giving are? If I am going to lay up treasures in Heaven, should I make any effort to see to it that my giving is making a difference?*

After taking some time to pray about this decision and then to investigate his options, Edward made a fantastic discovery. Not only was he able to make a difference with the $100 he had purposed to give; he could shake the world with it.

What Edward had discovered was an international ministry that was getting Bibles printed and distributed in one of the world's most populous nations. These Bibles were being given out in poverty-stricken areas where most of the people had never touched a Bible, let alone owned one. At the time, there was a tremendous revival going on in these areas, and as a result there was a tremendous hunger for the Word of God. Someone close to the situation had estimated that for each new Bible going into this country, at least two people would come to faith in Christ.

Even more amazing was the fact that the total cost for printing and distributing these Bibles was only $2 per copy. This meant Edward's $100 donation made it possible for fifty new Bibles to be distributed to hungry souls who had never owned a copy of God's Word.

With joy in his heart, with a prayer on his lips, and with visions of Christ's growing kingdom dancing in his head, Edward put his $100 in an envelope and dropped it in the mail.

This world would never be the same.

Elderly ladies who had prayed for decades that they could have their own copy of the Bible wept for joy as they saw their prayers come true.

Old men rejoiced as they heard, for the first time, the plan of salvation, and about how Christ had come to deliver them from the bondage of Satan.

Young women filled their villages with songs as they committed themselves, one by one, to the lordship of Christ.

Young men pledged their allegiance to the kingdom of God that they read about in His Word and committed themselves to work as missionaries to take the Gospel to the surrounding villages.

But it was not only the recipients of the Bibles who were changed by Edward's gift; he himself was being changed by what had just happened. His eyes seemed to be suddenly open to reality in a way that he had never seen it before. He began to daydream about God's kingdom and to fantasize about the harvest of souls in a way that made his pulse quicken and his heart race. Because of this one small act of giving, he was beginning to experience the truth of the words of Jesus, "Where your treasure is, there will your heart be also."

Chapter 9
Two Astounding Facts

As I look around me at the lives of the believers who live in the United States of America, there are two facts that astound me.

The first astounding fact is that virtually every one of us—even those with average jobs, average intelligence, and average training—has access to so many amazing opportunities to shake the world for Jesus and His kingdom.

The second astounding fact is that so few are making an honest effort to take advantage of these incredible opportunities.

What is it that is holding us back? For many Christians, it is the spirit of materialism, the "deceitfulness of riches," the drive to accumulate earthly wealth, which has blinded them to reality.

Many others, however, have recognized the deception of materialism and are actively fighting against it. Perhaps they have quit their lucrative jobs, downsized their possessions, and begun to live more simply. But they have still not developed a habit of serious and thoughtful charitable giving, or at least not one that is evident by looking at their check register. In other words, they have become convicted that they have too much stuff, but they have not yet embraced a vision of what they could do with that stuff.

Still other Christians have assented to the truth that giving is important and may have even gotten into the habit of dropping a donation into the offering basket every Sunday. Although this is not a particularly exciting activity for them, they still try to do it faithfully, because, after all, it seems like the right thing for a Christian to do.

But far too rare are the believers who have truly grasped the glorious privilege of giving and comprehended its astonishing potential. Far too many of us, sadly, have not yet had our imaginations captured and our visions stimulated with the realization that we hold in our hands the ability to powerfully impact the spiritual and physical needs of the world and to build God's kingdom in the process.

❧ ❧ ❧

If this book has one purpose, it is to inspire more of us to get into the battle, to slay giants, to tear down strongholds, to build Christ's kingdom. And it is to inspire us to make our pens and checkbooks key parts of our arsenal.

For this to happen, we need to inspire each other to be diligent like Brian, to be frugal like Caleb, and to be generous like David. But we need to inspire each other to do one more thing as well, and that is to be selective and purposeful in our giving. Because the truth is simply this: not all giving is created equal. As the contrast between David and Edward points out, some types of giving make more of a difference in God's kingdom than other types of giving.

My encouragement, therefore, is threefold:

1. Let us be joyfully generous in our giving.

2. Let us prayerfully examine our various opportunities for giving.

3. When possible, let us shift our giving more and more toward the opportunities that will make the most difference in God's kingdom.

Then when we go to sleep at night, we can rest with the confidence that our day of hard work has not been wasted.

We have been used by God to make a real difference. We have been used by God to build His kingdom. We have been used by God, in fact, to shake the world.

Chapter 10
Gifts That Grow

Still ecstatic about the impact he had been able to make with his first $100 gift, Edward began to think about the future. He was now more enthused than ever about practicing the diligence of Brian, the frugality of Caleb, and the generosity of David. As a result, it was not long until he was ready to give his second gift of $100. Once again, he wanted his gift to make a real difference in the lives of real people, and to point them to Jesus in the process.

His research turned up several promising leads, but one opportunity that especially caught his attention was a program called Gifts That Grow. This ministry delivered medicine and other material goods to impoverished people in third world countries. By taking advantage of corporate donations of surplus merchandise, this ministry was able to greatly multiply the impact of their donors, to the point where a donation of just $1 would result in well over $100 of medicine, clothing, and other items being distributed to needy people around the world.

Elatedly Edward wrote out his check and dropped it in the mail, still finding it hard to believe that he was able to impact so many lives with the meager "loaves and fishes" that he had to offer his Lord.

Chapter 11
Literature Subsidies

The weekend was approaching, and with it the Sunday morning service. Edward knew that there would be an offering lifted, as was usually done at his church, but he didn't know what the money would be going for.

After contacting his deacon and getting a list of the various offerings that would be taken that month, Edward discovered that the offering for this next Sunday was going to go to a ministry that subsidizes Bibles and other Christian literature going to various third world countries.

This ministry operated on a simple concept. It bought Bibles and Christian books at deep discounts, used donations received to lower the price even more, and then sold the literature at a loss to spiritually needy people in poor countries. The extremely low prices made it possible for people who otherwise would not be able to afford to buy the literature. But the fact that the recipients still paid at least a small amount ensured that the literature got into the hands of those who were genuinely interested in its message.

Edward was fascinated with the concept and gladly put his next $100 into the offering that Sunday. That afternoon, after doing some quick calculating to see how many people would likely be impacted by his donation, he spent some time praying that the soil of these hearts would be fertile and that there would be an abundance of fruit from the seeds that were about to be planted.

Chapter 12
The Weapon

That night Edward had a dream. He dreamed that he was part of a massive army advancing across a plain toward a huge fortress.

Within the fortress were millions of prisoners, held captive by their evil master Satan. Surrounding the fortress was a thick wall with a row of fortified doors; above the doors was emblazoned the caption "The Gates of Hell." The mission of those in the attacking army was to use their weaponry to break down the doors of the fortress and to free the prisoners within.

The Commander of the advancing army went from soldier to soldier, urging them to be courageous and handing out various weapons of warfare. To some he gave the weapon of preaching; to others, the weapon of prayer. To still others, he gave the weapon of fasting, or of exhorting, or of teaching, or of praise. Most of the soldiers were given more than one weapon, and they were all encouraged to use them valiantly.

One weapon the Commander handed to Edward, among others, was the weapon of giving. The Commander told him to take courage and to use his weapon with simplicity, with wisdom, and with patience.

Once every soldier had his weapons in hand and the order was given to advance, the liberating army sprang into action, every weapon blazing. With every new barrage of artillery, the walls would shudder, the gates would crack open, and a few more prisoners would escape to freedom.

The battle would prove to be long, hard, and costly for the liberating army. However, with every soldier fighting valiantly, under the leadership of their invincible Commander, the gates of Hell never stood a chance.

Chapter 13
More Literature

As Edward contemplated the dream he had just had, he realized the powerful truth that it represented. He, in fact, was a part of a mighty army, the army of God, which was waging war against the hosts of Satan and wickedness. Their leader was King Jesus, who had commanded them to attack the fortress holding the slaves of sin, "to turn them from darkness to light, and from the power of Satan unto God, that they may receive forgiveness of sins, and inheritance among them which are sanctified by faith that is in me."

"How can I best use this weapon of giving to do the maximum damage to Satan's kingdom?" Edward kept asking himself. His experience with the literature subsidies had set his imagination churning about the incredible potency of launching large quantities of Christian literature deep into enemy territory. Once again, he began to investigate his options.

Soon he discovered a ministry that printed small booklets containing various portions of God's Word. These Scripture booklets had been translated into hundreds of the most widely used languages of the world. They were then given free of charge to various Christian ministries, who in turn took them all over the world and distributed them to those who sat in spiritual darkness.

The amazing thing about these booklets was the incredible efficiency at which they were being produced. Labor costs were kept low through the sacrifices of the paid employees as well as the donated labor from work teams from local congregations. Material costs were reduced by buying bulk quantities of ink, paper, and other needed items. Because of this efficiency, a donation of just one dollar would result in twenty-five of these booklets being sent to a spiritually hungry part of this world.

Upon making this discovery, Edward did not hesitate a moment. He quickly pulled his weapon to his shoulder, took careful aim, and fired. As the blast of the shot reverberated through the surrounding hills, the enemy forces could do nothing but duck for cover, grit their fangs, and shudder.

എ എ എ

After pausing just long enough to reload, Edward quickly resumed his hunt for a worthy target. Digging through a stack of newsletters sitting on his desk, he realized he had struck gold when he unearthed a ministry printing small Bible storybooks. These booklets contained a Gospel presentation in the back, and each one-dollar donation would result in four of these high-quality booklets going into a needy third world country.

Edward was especially excited after he read stories about what was happening to the books when they arrived in the destination country. Desiring to get these powerful booklets into the hands of the maximum number of people, the missionaries would request permission to go into grade schools and pass out the booklets to the children in the schools. The children received these gifts gladly and then took them home to their parents, many of whom lived in some of the most remote villages of the country.

Once again, Edward couldn't wait to respond. As excited as a new hunter with a case of buck fever, he quickly aimed again and fired. Even from this distance, he knew instinctively that he had hit the target dead center.

ↀ   ↀ   ↀ

Until now, most of the literature Edward had funded had ended up in places outside his home country. Although joyfully grateful for these opportunities, he began to wonder whether he could make a similar impact through literature in his own nation.

Then a visiting speaker to his church gave a talk about the hundreds of thousands of men and women behind bars in this country. The tremendous spiritual needs in prisons quickly grabbed Edward's attention.

The speaker told about a Christian magazine published especially for prisoners, and how many lives had already been changed as they read the articles and testimonies in it. He told about the tremendous spiritual hunger among prisoners, and how one magazine is often passed from person to person and read multiple times until it is completely worn-out.

The speaker told of the growing demand for the magazine and how prisoners and chaplains all over the country were requesting subscriptions. He told how the current demand far outstripped the supply, and that the circulation could be greatly expanded if only more funds were available. And he told how a donation of just fifty cents would put one more magazine into the hands of another needy prisoner.

For the third time that week, Edward fired his weapon, and the results were amazing. Centuries earlier, during the days of Paul and Silas, a prison had been shaken, captives had been freed, and souls had been saved. It now appeared, at least to some extent, that history was repeating itself.

Chapter 14
Put Your Money Into the Message

Writing sometime in the first half of the 1900s, Oswald J. Smith, a Canadian pastor and writer, challenged believers to put their money into the Gospel of Jesus Christ rather than into luxurious houses of worship. Here is what he wrote.

> We must decide whether we are going to put our money into the building, or into the message. For nearly 1900 years now, the church has been putting its money into the building; and, instead of getting out the message, we have been erecting magnificent and luxurious auditoriums in which to worship God.

> Some false cults have been much wiser. They put their money into their erroneous message.

They know that the message is more important than the building. Yet all over the United States of America and the Dominion of Canada we are still investing in bricks and mortar, whereas God wants us to invest in the message.

Not until the church realizes that the message is more important than the building will we be able to evangelize the world. If for every fourteen cents invested in the "printed page" we can win a soul for Christ, then by all means we should put our money into the message.

God did not tell us to build luxurious churches and invite the people to come in. He told us to go out with the message and preach the Gospel to the entire world. Let us put our money not into the building, but into the message.[1]

---

1 Smith, Oswald J., *The Challenge of Missions*.

Chapter 15
The Nameless Girl

One day Edward read the following story:

The temperature was 103°, with very little wind. The land lay barren in all directions, with no trees, plants, or food in sight. In the middle of this desert stood a small shelter, six feet wide, eight feet long, and just tall enough to sit under. This plastic tent didn't do much for shade, but rather worked like an oven, elevating the inside temperature even more. This tent was not the only one of its kind; there were rows and rows of similar structures, stretching endlessly in all directions.

Inside this lonely tent, lost in a jungle of other makeshift buildings, was a dusty mat. On this mat lay a girl: a dirty, dehydrated, and nameless six-year-old girl. Along with her, the tent was home to a host of flies, beetles, and other small things that buzzed. The girl lay motionless on her mat, slowly breathing deep, pain-filled breaths. The only sounds other than her heavy breathing and the buzz of little creatures were the distant cries of others in similar situations.

The body temperature of this young, nameless girl was about the same as the stagnant air around her. Her body ached. She felt nauseated. This small, nameless girl had not been born with a defect; she did not have terminal cancer. Her situation was the direct result of war.

Her father had been threatened, attacked, and killed in her home country, leaving her mother alone with the children. Soon after that, her mother died, leaving her, this nameless girl, an orphan. She and her neighbors had fled her country and everything she knew to come to this barren place with its rows upon rows of plastic tents.

On their way she had contracted a disease from drinking brown water out of a pool in the middle of the desert. This disease would have been easily curable with a little medicine and clean water to drink. But the needed medicine was miles away, and any water that was closer than that was not clean. (Actually, there was clean water much closer, but between this girl and the lifesaving liquid was fifty feet of dirt and rock.)

As this young, nameless, and desperately sick girl lay on her dusty mat, she remembered what her mother had told her about the God of love, and about His Son Jesus, who had the power to give her lifesaving water. As she pondered this thought, she cried out to Him, the One who could save her. And as she lay dying in her plastic hut, this Jesus responded to her plea. He told her that he loved her and had servants in a faraway land whom He had greatly blessed with material prosperity. He told her that He had called these servants to be His hands and feet in this world, and that He would use these blessings to save her life.

≈ ≈ ≈

As Edward read, he was moved with compassion for the girl. He knew that people all over the world struggled to stay alive in situations just like these. He had learned that around the world there were people dying from curable diseases every few seconds. And he knew that he could be God's tool to save the life of at least a few like this girl. Some of his friends thought that since his little would save only a tiny percentage of the world's dying children, he shouldn't even try to save any. But Edward knew what Jesus would have done while on the earth if *He* had the opportunity to help such a girl.

Chapter 16
Seeds

As time went on, Edward grew more and more passionate about laying up treasures in Heaven and about shaking the world for Jesus in the process. He discovered opportunities to show God's love to needy people all over the world. Sometimes this was through food boxes for the hungry, sometimes through bundles of clothing for the naked, and sometimes through water sources for the thirsty. At times the help went to widows and orphans, at other times to victims of natural disasters, and at still other times to refugees fleeing from persecution or war. Nearly every time, Edward came away amazed at what a profound difference he could make for $100 or less.

One day a friend told Edward about project in which a Christian ministry was distributing garden seeds to needy families. These seeds were given out in poverty-stricken areas where high-quality seeds were not readily available; therefore, these seeds were received eagerly and nearly all of them were put to use.

Edward immediately fell in love with this project for a variety of reasons. First of all, this type of giving did not carry with it much of the downside of pure handouts, in that the recipients had to do substantial work themselves in order to reap the benefits of the gift. Second, as the seeds were distributed from village to village, public meetings were held, not only to give out the seeds, but also to share a Gospel message. And third, a donation of just $100 was enough to provide seeds to sixty families and had the potential to produce enough vegetables to fill four semitrucks!

As Edward considered the impact his small gift would make, he thought again of the words of Jesus Christ, who said, "Inasmuch as ye have done it unto one of the least of these my brethren, ye have done it unto me."

Chapter 17
The Grief Letter

Several years ago I received a newsletter from a ministry in a distant state. This ministry had a vision to supply audio messages and Gospel tracts to needy souls in the United States and around the world. At the time of this newsletter, it had been actively engaged in sending Gospel literature overseas for several decades.

What struck me about this newsletter was an enclosed note from the correspondence secretary of the ministry. After briefly describing the operations of the organization and her duties in it, she shared her own heartache over the many pleas that she receives for Gospel materials and Bibles.

She shared numerous quotes from Christian leaders in countries such as Kenya, Zambia, Nigeria, Cameroon, and Malawi, who told how God was using their Gospel literature to touch many lives. These leaders were requesting more literature, expressing their desire to use it to win many souls "before the soon return of Jesus Christ."

The secretary's heartache came, not from the encouraging testimonies, but from the stark fact that the ministry simply did not have the funds necessary to fulfill these requests. Although the literature was already printed and even put into boxes, it often then sat in those boxes for many months, waiting for enough funds to come in so that they could be shipped.

Rather than sending out the boxes of literature, therefore, the secretary instead was forced to send this reply (slightly edited), which she called her "grief" letter, to the many requests that were coming in.

> Dear Friend:
>
> Greetings of Christian love come to you today in the wonderful name of Jesus.
>
> Thank you for your recent letter. We are sorry you have not received a parcel from us. LET ME EXPLAIN... This ministry is a faith work. By faith, we believe God does provide. We do not go into debt to purchase materials. A large amount of money is needed to purchase an order

of tracts in quantity. Once these are paid, then additional funds are needed to mail the materials. (We are working in more than thirty African countries along with other parts of the world.)

At this time our director is sending boxes of Gospel materials that were requested up to eight months ago. The costs to mail our boxes has risen to be very expensive. We are grieved with the inability to promise anything more to anyone until we catch up on present letters. We have boxes ready to mail but lack funds for postage. We include one Bible in each box along with the tracts.

Our hearts' desire is to provide all of the materials that are asked for. But we cannot. We are much in prayer about this. Please pray for this ministry.

We praise God for all the work you are continuing to do for Him. Let us always keep faithful to our LORD JESUS.

Sincerely,
Correspondence Secretary

Upon reading this "grief letter," I was struck with the amazing opportunity sitting in the laps of any of us who happened to have a little extra cash sitting around. My plea to those around me then was the same as it is today:

> I'm sending you the attached investment opportunity by e-mail. And as far as I can tell by reading it, it clearly qualifies as one amazing example of how we can shake this world with nothing more than a stamp, an envelope, a pen, and one hundred dollars.

> A few days ago I received the attached letter from [ministry's name], a ministry that has been sending literature overseas for quite a number of years. As I read the letter, it struck me immediately that this was something I wanted to share with the rest of you as well. Be especially sure to read the pleas for literature on page 2, and then the letter of reply on page 3 that explains why they are eight months behind in the mailings. Two things struck me as I read it. (1) The tremendous difference we can make with a little bit of money, and (2) The tremendous tragedy it would be if we let this opportunity get away from us.

As you can see if you've read the attachment, nearly all the pieces are already in place for a successful evangelism campaign. Hungry souls? They're there. Willing evangelists? Ready and waiting. Prayer support? Happening as we speak. Gospel materials? Printed and ready to go. The only thing missing? The money to ship the literature overseas.

So go shake the world for Jesus. It will take you two and a half minutes.

In the investing world, shrewd money managers keep their eyes open for those once-in-a-lifetime investment opportunities in which a small amount of money can be used to generate a large return, preferably in a short period of time, and preferably with very little risk. How much more should we as members of God's kingdom be alert to opportunities to invest in heavenly treasure, especially when we can make such a tremendous impact with so little.

Chapter 18
Microloans, Macro Impact

As Edward continued to look for ways to give to the needy around the world, he became especially interested in methods that would give long-term help rather than create a dependency mentality. One avenue that especially caught his attention was the concept of microloans.

Although the different microloan ministries operate in a variety of methods, their basic goal is to provide small amounts of capital to individuals in third world countries to enable them to start or expand their own small businesses. This concept, when administered effectively, has repeatedly proven to be one of the most efficient ways to help poor people break the cycle of poverty in which they have been trapped.

Often microloans are made in conjunction with a Bible-based teaching program. They are often made at little or no interest and stipulate that the principal be paid back within a short period of time, perhaps one year or less. Then these paid-back funds are loaned out again under similar arrangements. Thus the same money can be used multiple times to change lives over and over again.

After the business owner receives his loan, he might use the money to purchase additional inventory or to buy a tool to help the business operate more efficiently. Whatever the case, testimonies abound about how a very small loan (often less than $50 U.S.) has been instrumental in jump-starting a small business to the point where it was able to support a family.

Obviously, we are talking here about an economy where the cost of living is low, the scale of business operations is small, and the fixed expenses of doing business are negligible. In such an environment, what seems to us like a very small loan can increase a business's operations by a large percentage, and thus make a major difference in the lives of the owners.

Giving through microloans encourages the poor to break out of the cycle of poverty, not by relying on handouts, but rather by the dignity of their own hard work. It is a great illustration of the proverb, "Give a man a fish, and you feed him for a day. Teach a man to fish, and you feed him for a lifetime."

This concept impressed Edward immensely, and he began to search for solid, Christ-centered organizations that operate efficient microloan ministries. The thought struck him that, just maybe, he had finally found a way to put into practice the mysterious command of Jesus to "lend, hoping for nothing again."

Chapter 19
The Windows

In 2006 I wrote Through the Eye of a Needle, *a book about what I called the doctrine of nonaccumulation—that is, Jesus' teachings about laying up treasures in Heaven rather than on earth. Receiving feedback from readers, I sensed that some were struggling to understand and to catch the vision I hoped they would catch. I wrote an article entitled "The Windows," and began sharing it with those who contacted me with questions. Here is an edited version of it.*

In the months since *Through the Eye of a Needle* was first offered for sale, the response has been tremendous. Many people have written, expressing appreciation for the book and its message. However, many still have questions. Honest-hearted people wonder how Jesus' teachings about economics ought to apply in their lives. What exactly are they to do with

Luke 12:33? What about this asset I own, this situation I face, or this opportunity I have?

I sympathize with those who face these struggles. I have faced, and still face, many of them myself. Nor can I answer all these questions for you. I will, however, tell you a story that might help you grasp at least part of Jesus' message and answer these questions for yourself.

෴   ෴   ෴

Two men become convicted about Jesus' teaching on economics. Both are convinced that Jesus' commands to "sell and give" and "do not lay up treasures on earth" are meant to be taken literally. They both set out with a firm determination to find a way to obey these commands.

Each of these men owns a home along the shore of a great ocean. Both houses have only two windows, one that overlooks the ocean, and the other that gives a view into the basement where all his earthly possessions are kept.

The first man goes immediately to the basement window. After pasting his nose to the glass for some time, he reaches down, grabs a handful of money, and announces to his wife, "Honey, I think we have too many possessions. Please take this money and give it away."

"Okay," says his wife. "Where do you want me to send it?"

"Oh, I don't care," the man responds. "Just go get rid of it somewhere."

He returns to the basement window, and after more contemplation, decides that he still has too many assets. He reaches down, grabs another handful of money, and instructs his wife to give that away too. Where? "I don't care. Just send it away so that it's not in our basement anymore."

He returns to the window and repeats the process several times.

That night he cannot sleep. The first hour he lies awake wondering if he still has too much wealth and should give away more. The next hour he wonders if he has given away too much and if maybe he doesn't need to take Christ's commands quite so literally. After all, what will happen to me if I get sick? or old? or tired of working?

The second man also determines to put his convictions into practice. He, however, goes to the ocean-view window and picks up his binoculars. Peering out over the ocean, he suddenly calls out to his wife, "Honey, look at all the people over there who are starving! Quick, let's send them some money for food." His wife reaches into the basement and gives him a handful of cash, which he quickly sends across the ocean.

He shifts his gaze a little to the right. "And over there in that country, people don't have adequate clothes or shelter or medicine! Let's send them as much as we can right away. And over here are some pastors who need Bibles, and here are some missionaries who need tracts, and here's a native pastor we can support while he preaches to an unreached tribe! Wow, what wonderful opportunities! Quick, hand me some more money to send."

This continues all afternoon, until his wife finally announces, "There isn't any more money."

With his eyes still glued to the binoculars, he responds urgently, "Then sell something! Let's get the money wherever we can! There are still so many opportunities; and if we wait, we might miss them forever!"

Going to bed that night, he's as happy and excited as he has ever been. His mind is full of thoughts of people who have food in their stomachs, clothes on their backs, a Bible in their hands, and Jesus in their hearts, all because he gave! He can't wait to get up the next morning, go to work, earn more money, and do it all over again.

☙ ☙ ☙

As you consider Jesus' commands to "sell and give" and "lay not up for yourselves treasures upon earth," does your mind go first to the basement window or to the ocean-view window?

Both men, in a sense, obeyed the commandment of Christ. Both responses showed they wanted to take Christ seriously. But one slept much better than the other.

You see, our journey through the eye of a needle will be far more enjoyable, and probably more successful, if we fix our gaze out the ocean window instead of through the basement window.

How can we actually do this? What are some practical steps we can take to tear our gaze away from the basement window and put it on the ocean window?

Here is one practical suggestion: subscribe to the newsletters of organizations that are feeding the hungry, clothing the naked, ministering to the sick, distributing Christian literature, and preaching the Gospel of Jesus Christ. Take time to read them and to pray for the needs they describe. Doing this, we will be amazed at the opportunities we have available to lay up treasure in Heaven. As we turn our attention toward Christ and the needs in His body, we'll find that "the things of earth will grow strangely dim"[1] and our affections will migrate more and more toward those things that are above.

> "Lift up your eyes, and look on
> the fields…" – John 4:35

---

1 Lemmel, Helen H., "*Turn your Eyes Upon Jesus,*" 1922.

Chapter 20
Native Evangelists

The Gospel of Jesus Christ is the most life-changing message this world has ever known. Ever since Christ gave His Great Commission, His disciples have been working to take the Gospel to those who have never heard it.

Here in America, we often think of this missionary enterprise in terms of messengers from the United States and Canada traveling to countries that have less of a Gospel witness. And truly God has used this model to reach many souls for Him.

However, this traditional approach has several problems. First, the cost to send an American missionary overseas can often be more than $50,000 per year. Second, the American missionary will usually have some sort of language barrier to overcome before he can communicate the Gospel to an unreached group. Third, there are usually numerous barriers relating to culture, climate, and health that can take a foreign missionary years to overcome.

In response to these problems with this approach, numerous mission organizations have chosen instead to work with native Christians in their target country, helping them to evangelize their own people. Sometimes this is done by supplying resources to existing missions in these countries. Other times it is done by supporting individual pastors or evangelists so that they can spend all their time in evangelization and ministry.

The result is that the cost to put one missionary on the field drops from thousands of dollars each month to just hundreds. These native workers can often live far more cheaply than their counterparts from America. Not only that, the costs for travel and furloughs are far less, if they exist at all. The net result is that the average cost per worker can be a tiny fraction of what it would be for an American worker.

But perhaps even more importantly, the native workers usually do not face the language and cultural barriers an American missionary faces. They often speak the same language, and speak it in the same way as the people they are trying to reach, without going to expensive and time-consuming language school. They understand local customs much better than a foreign missionary would, and therefore are less likely to cause offense by a careless word or action.

After reading several books introducing, describing, and promoting the effectiveness of native ministries, Edward decided to help support one, then two, and eventually three workers in foreign countries. He had always had a heart for foreign missions and had thought that someday he might go overseas himself, but now he was amazed by how much he could do to build God's kingdom by staying home, working hard, and supplying funds to send others. He also prayed regularly for the three missionaries he supported and took great comfort in the fact that they also prayed for him.

Chapter 21
Planting in Plowed Soil

In the parable of the sower, Jesus told about the differences between "soils" and the different ways in which they received the Word of God. Scripture also tells us about stony and hard hearts and indicates that such people are unlikely to respond positively to the Gospel. Many of us, especially those of us who live in wealthy, politically stable countries such as the United States, can testify to the difficulty of trying to share the Gospel with those who feel safe, comfortable, and satisfied with where they are.

The good news is that God has His ways to "plow" the hard soil of human hearts to make them more receptive to the message of Jesus. These "plows" are usually painful experiences of some kind, such as persecution, poverty, war, disease, or natural disasters. Although these painful experiences in some cases have made people bitter toward God, at other times they have softened proud hearts and opened the door for repentance and salvation.

As Edward saw reports in the news about suffering caused by famines, earthquakes, hurricanes, political upheaval, disease, and refugee crises, he realized these were things a merciful God allowed in order to draw men and women to Himself. He began to see such events as opportunities to sow the good seed of the Word into hearts that were more receptive than average.

He began to research ministries that specialized in helping victims of persecution, war, and natural disasters. Sometimes these ministries give physical aid such as food, medicine, clothing, or housing. Other times they focused on spiritual aid such as Bibles and Christian literature. Edward was especially excited about ministries that did both, ministering to the physical needs as described in Matthew 25 as well as sharing the Gospel as commanded in Matthew 28.

Chapter 22
Principles of Giving (Investing)

Amy Carmichael said, "You can give without loving, but you cannot love without giving." To those of you who are serious about putting love for Jesus into action through a life of giving, here are a few basic principles to consider.

Principle 1 – Give Where God's Heart Is

Throughout Scripture we see the truth that our God has a heart for the poor and needy in the world. He continually commands His people to look out for the widows, the orphans, the sick, and the hungry. He says that true religion, in part, is that which looks out for these people (James 1:27). He also declares that on Judgment Day we will largely be judged by how we have responded to such physical needs (Matthew 25).

God also has a heart for His Gospel to be preached through the whole world. Christ's final commands to His disciples were to "go ye therefore, and teach all nations" and to "preach the gospel to every creature." He told His followers that He would make them "fishers of men," and charged them to pray "the Lord of the harvest, that he would send forth labourers into his harvest."

Since God's primary passions are helping the poor and spreading the Gospel, should not we as born-again Christians make these issues our passions as well? Should not our giving reflect that these things are our passions? Would it not be good to examine our giving to see what percentage of our giving is going toward accomplishing these two great passions of God?

Principle 2 – Give With True Christian Love

Jesus said that the two greatest commands are to love God with all our heart, soul, mind, and strength; and to love our neighbor as ourselves. In 1 Corinthians 13 Paul writes that even if we were to give all our possessions to feed the poor, it would not profit us anything if it were done without love.

Let us examine our love for God and our love for others and ask ourselves whether godly charity is truly the foundational motive for our giving.

Principle 3 – Give Only What Is Really Ours

This is another way of saying that we should make sure our obligations are met before we engage in freewill giving. When we have bills we are obligated to pay, that money is not really ours to give. It belongs to someone else, and it would be a form of stealing to use it for something voluntary while neglecting to stay current with our financial obligations, whatever they are.

So as wonderful as it would be to give away a large portion of this month's paycheck, it is important to first pause and ask a few questions. Am I current on my financial obligations such as rent expense, car payments, and utility bills? Am I meeting my legal obligations, such as maintaining my car insurance and paying my income taxes? Have I contributed my fair share to my local congregation for its operating expenses and ongoing programs?

Once I have taken care of my minimum obligations to others, then I will have a clearer picture of how much I have left that I am free to invest in Christ's kingdom.

Principle 4 – Diversify Our Giving

Ecclesiastes 11:2 says, "Give a portion to seven, and also to eight; for thou knowest not what evil shall be upon the earth."

Some Christian financial advisors use this verse to promote the diversification of accumulated earthly assets. I suggest instead that we take this verse as a motivation to diversify our giving.

Suppose we choose to channel all our charitable giving into one organization and later discover it had been misusing, mishandling, or misappropriating the funds that had been donated to it (an occurrence that is sadly all too common). How would we feel then? Would it seem like all our giving had been in vain? But if we've done our research and are giving to a number of worthy programs and one of them "goes bad," we can still rejoice that the majority of our giving is being used in a worthy, kingdom-building way.

Principle 5 – Give Sacrificially

Once we have grasped the power, the privilege, and the potential in giving, we will be looking for opportunities to put it into practice.

Jesus has graciously given us a wonderful tool, which for many people could be the most potent way to free up money to give. This tool was given by way of His command to "sell and give" in Luke 12:33. Obeying this command can often open doors of opportunity that are many times greater than any other method of raising money we might have.

Barnabas put this command into practice in Acts 4:37 when he sold a piece of land in order to give. Others of us might not have an extra piece of land sitting around, but perhaps we have some savings accounts or certificates of deposit we could cash in. Or maybe we have attics full of "treasures" that could be turned into cash through a well-organized garage sale.

Is this command in Luke 12:33, then, only for those who are rich? What about those of us who don't have many earthly assets at all, let alone an unused piece of prime real estate like Barnabas? Are we destined to miss out on the blessings of obedience to this verse?

No, we also have the privilege of obeying this verse. How? By selling the most valuable asset we own, which for many of us is our time. Every day God graciously deposits into our account the gift of twenty-four hours. Since there is no cost for these hours, however many of them we can sell before they expire results in a 100 percent profit margin!

Paul's instructions for the converted thief are to "labour, working with his hands the thing which is good, that he may have to give to him that needeth" (Ephesians 4:28). Not only will this help break his bondage to his past sins, it will also make a real difference to needy people. And he will be storing up heavenly treasures for himself in the process!

Jesus taught that when we choose to sacrifice something of ours in order to build God's kingdom, we "shall receive an hundredfold, and shall inherit everlasting life."

Principle 6 – Give Secretly

In Matthew 6 Jesus commanded that when we give to the needy, we should do it in secret rather than in public. He knew how deceptive the human heart can be and how quickly we can begin to do things out of a desire for personal recognition.

This wrong motive, a desire for the praise of men, is the devil's counterfeit to the true, godly motive for giving, as described in Principle 2. To combat this counterfeit, Jesus simply told us to do our giving in secret. If we do this, then God, who sees what is done in secret, will reward us openly.

Principle 7 – Give Cheerfully

In 2 Corinthians 9:7 Paul says we ought to give "not grudgingly, or of necessity: for God loveth a cheerful giver."

What makes the difference between a grudging giver and a cheerful giver? Most of the time, it is simply a difference in vision. Unlike the grudging giver, the cheerful giver has grasped a clear vision of what is really happening when he gives.

The cheerful giver has a vision of the truth that it is more blessed to give than to receive. He sees by faith that every dollar he gives is not gone; it is going into a heavenly bank account with his name on it. And he has a vision of the truth that if he is careful about where he gives his money, he can change many lives and shake the world for Jesus.

With all those truths so clear in his vision, how could he not be cheerful?

Chapter 23

Still More
Opportunities

As Edward continued his investigations, he continued to discover amazing ways to shake the world with a relatively small amount of money.

One of them involved providing sponsorships for school-age students in a poorer country. This country had many private schools, as well as many children who needed schooling. But the education system was still in a sad condition due to the suffocating poverty that pervaded everything.

By donating only ten dollars a month, Edward was able to provide a life-changing education for a child who would otherwise have to do without. This money, though not much by American standards, was enough to provide basic text-books, Christ-based training for the teachers, and one meal per day for the student (which might be the only meal he would receive that day).

Another opportunity that seemed to have amazing potential was a ministry that provided wells and other clean water sources to villages that previously had access only to polluted water. Many of these people had never heard the Gospel of Jesus, but when they came from the surrounding countryside to receive free water, they would also be introduced to the source of living water, Jesus Christ. Edward could see that by providing financial help toward these projects, he was putting into place some valuable resources that would keep on giving the love of Christ, both physically and spiritually, for years to come.

හ හ හ

Okay, I know what some of you are saying by now, *That's not fair—you're not sticking to your book title. Edward may be shaking the world in many ways, but he's using a lot more than one hundred dollars to do it.*

And you're right, of course.

But don't you see? That's the way joyful giving for the Lord's sake works. When a disciple of Jesus gets hold of the reality of what his money can do, he doesn't stop with the first hundred dollars. He can't. He just keeps on giving, just as his Lord gave and keeps on giving.

"Freely ye have received, freely give."
– Matthew 10:8

Chapter 24
Pressing Toward the Mark

As time went on, and as Edward grew older, he was occasionally tempted to slack off in his life of radical giving. He sometimes wondered whether it would do any harm, really, if he would just cut back a little in his diligence in work or in his frugality in spending. Would there be anything wrong with reducing the treasures he was laying up in Heaven so that he could instead lay up some treasures on earth?

But then he would remember the commands of his beloved Master. He would remember the promises associated with those commands. He would recall that Jesus had said, "If ye love me, keep my commandments." He would remember God's faithfulness in the past to supply all his needs.

But with special enthusiasm Edward would think about the multitudes of needy people in the world and how obeying

Christ's commands had given him the ability to make a real difference in so many of their lives. He would remember once again the incredible opportunity he had to show Christ's love, to build God's kingdom, and to shake the world for Jesus.

And so, with a grateful heart, Edward would always press on with his calling, "not grudgingly, or of necessity," but with absolute cheerfulness as he rejoiced in the tremendous privileges he had so graciously been given.

Afterword

O God in Heaven, please raise up a whole army of people who are passionate about building God's kingdom with whatever tools You have given them.

Raise up people who have learned to work hard and manage their finances well, not so they can accumulate wealth on earth, but rather so they can lay up treasures in Heaven.

Raise up people who have crucified the covetousness of their own hearts and have caught a vision of what can be done by letting go of the temporal riches of this world in exchange for the eternal riches in Heaven. Please use them to spread the Gospel, to feed the hungry, to build Your kingdom, to shake the world.

For Jesus' sake. Amen.

If you have questions or comments about this book, the author invites you to contact him through the publisher:

Roger Hertzler

c/o Christian Light

P.O. Box 1212

Harrisonburg, VA 22803

info@christianlight.org

Christian Light is a nonprofit, conservative Mennonite publishing company providing Christ-centered, Biblical literature including books, Gospel tracts, Sunday school materials, summer Bible school materials, and a full curriculum for Christian day schools and homeschools. Though produced primarily in English, some books, tracts, and school materials are also available in Spanish.

For more information about the ministry of Christian Light or its publications, or for spiritual help, please contact us at:

ADDRESS :: P. O. Box 1212,
Harrisonburg, VA 22803

TELEPHONE :: 540-434-0768

FAX :: 540-433-8896

E-MAIL :: info@christianlight.org

WEBSITE :: www.christianlight.org

CHRISTIAN LIGHT

PUBLICATIONS